Betty the Toolmaker!

Supersmart Crow

BY SARAH EASON
ILLUSTRATED BY DIEGO VAISBERG

BEARPORT
PUBLISHING

Minneapolis, Minnesota

BEAR CLAW

Credits: 20, © Rudra Narayan Mitra/Shutterstock; 21, © Paul Reeves Photography/Shutterstock; 22, © Melanie Hobson/Shutterstock; 23, © Sandra Standbridge/Shutterstock.

Bearport Publishing Company Product Development Team
President: Jen Jenson; Director of Product Development: Spencer Brinker; Senior Editor: Allison Juda; Editor: Charly Haley; Associate Editor: Naomi Reich; Senior Designer: Colin O'Dea; Associate Designer: Elena Klinkner; Associate Designer: Kayla Eggert; Product Development Assistant: Anita Stasson

Produced by Calcium
Editor: Jennifer Sanderson; Proofreader: Harriet McGregor; Designer: Paul Myerscough; Picture Researcher: Rachel Blount

DISCLAIMER: This graphic story is a dramatization based on true events. It is intended to give the reader a sense of the narrative rather than a presentation of actual details as they occurred.

Library of Congress Cataloging-in-Publication Data

Names: Eason, Sarah, author. | Vaisberg, Diego, illustrator.
Title: Betty the toolmaker! : supersmart crow / by Sarah Eason ; illustrated by Diego Vaisberg.
Description: Bear Claw books. | Minneapolis, Minnesota : Bearport Publishing Company, [2023] | Series: Animal masterminds | Includes bibliographical references and index.
Identifiers: LCCN 2022033458 (print) | LCCN 2022033459 (ebook) | ISBN 9798885094290 (library binding) | ISBN 9798885095518 (paperback) | ISBN 9798885096669 (ebook)
Subjects: LCSH: Crows--Behavior--Juvenile literature. | Crows--Behavior--Comic books, strips, etc. | Animal intelligence--Juvenile literature. | Animal intelligence--Comic books, strips, etc. | Learning in animals--Juvenile literature. | Learning in animals--Comic books, strips, etc. | Tool use in animals--Juvenile literature. | Tool use in animals--Comic books, strips, etc. | LCGFT: Graphic novels.
Classification: LCC QL696.P2367 E27 2023 (print) | LCC QL696.P2367 (ebook) | DDC 598.8/6415--dc23/eng/20220829
LC record available at https://lccn.loc.gov/2022033458
LC ebook record available at https://lccn.loc.gov/2022033459

For more information, write to Bearport Publishing, 5357 Penn Avenue South, Minneapolis, MN 55419.

Contents

CHAPTER 1

A Startling Discovery 4

CHAPTER 2

Betty and Abel 8

CHAPTER 3

Smart Crows................... 14

All about Crows.................... 20

More Smart Crows................22

Glossary 23

Index 24

Read More 24

Learn More Online....................24

CHAPTER 1

CHAPTER I

A Startling Discovery

In 2002, Oxford University **researcher** Alex Kacelnik had just heard of some exciting new animal behavior.

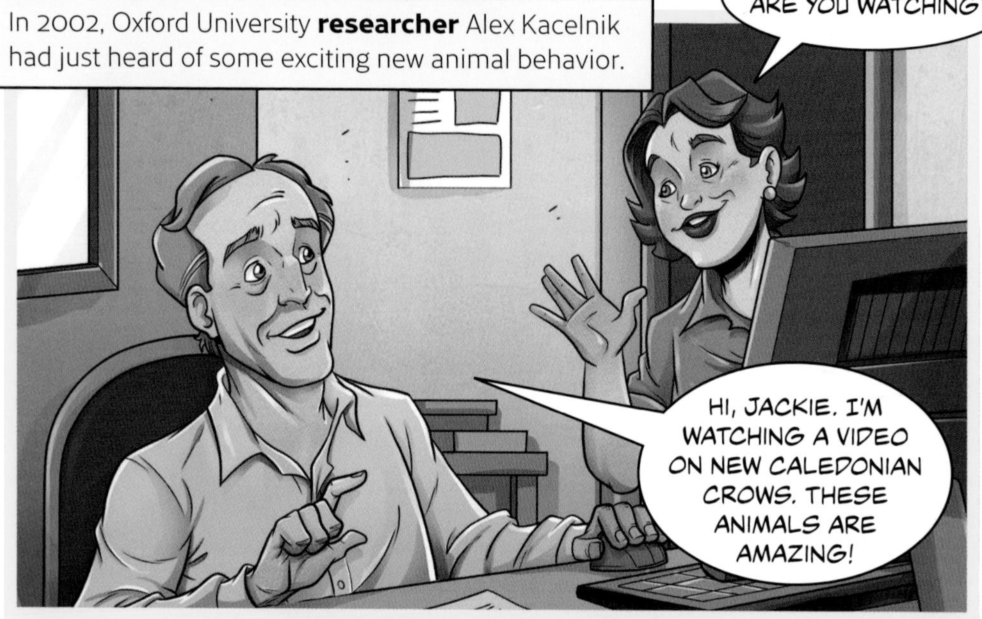
HI, ALEX. WHAT ARE YOU WATCHING?
HI, JACKIE. I'M WATCHING A VIDEO ON NEW CALEDONIAN CROWS. THESE ANIMALS ARE AMAZING!

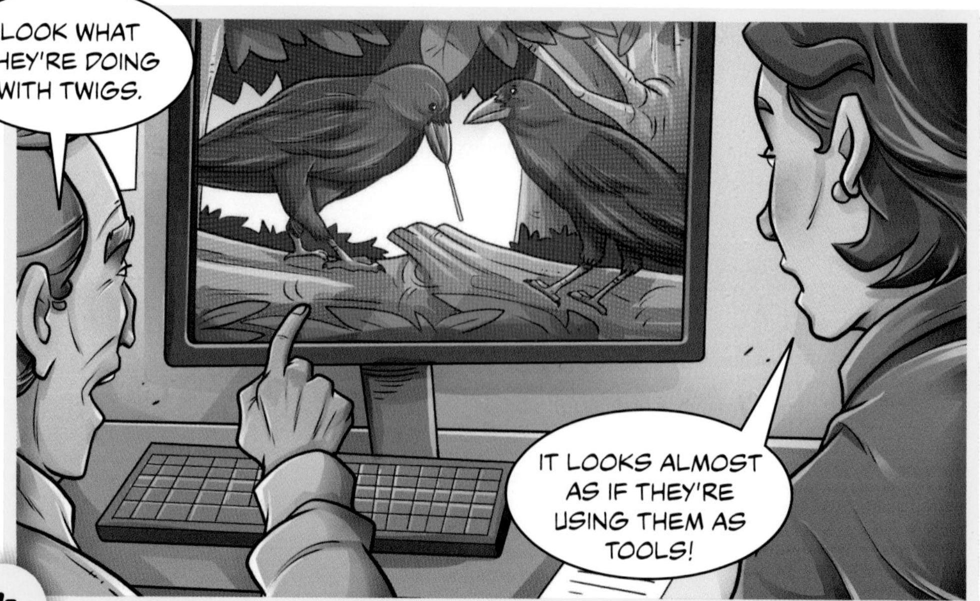
LOOK WHAT THEY'RE DOING WITH TWIGS.
IT LOOKS ALMOST AS IF THEY'RE USING THEM AS TOOLS!

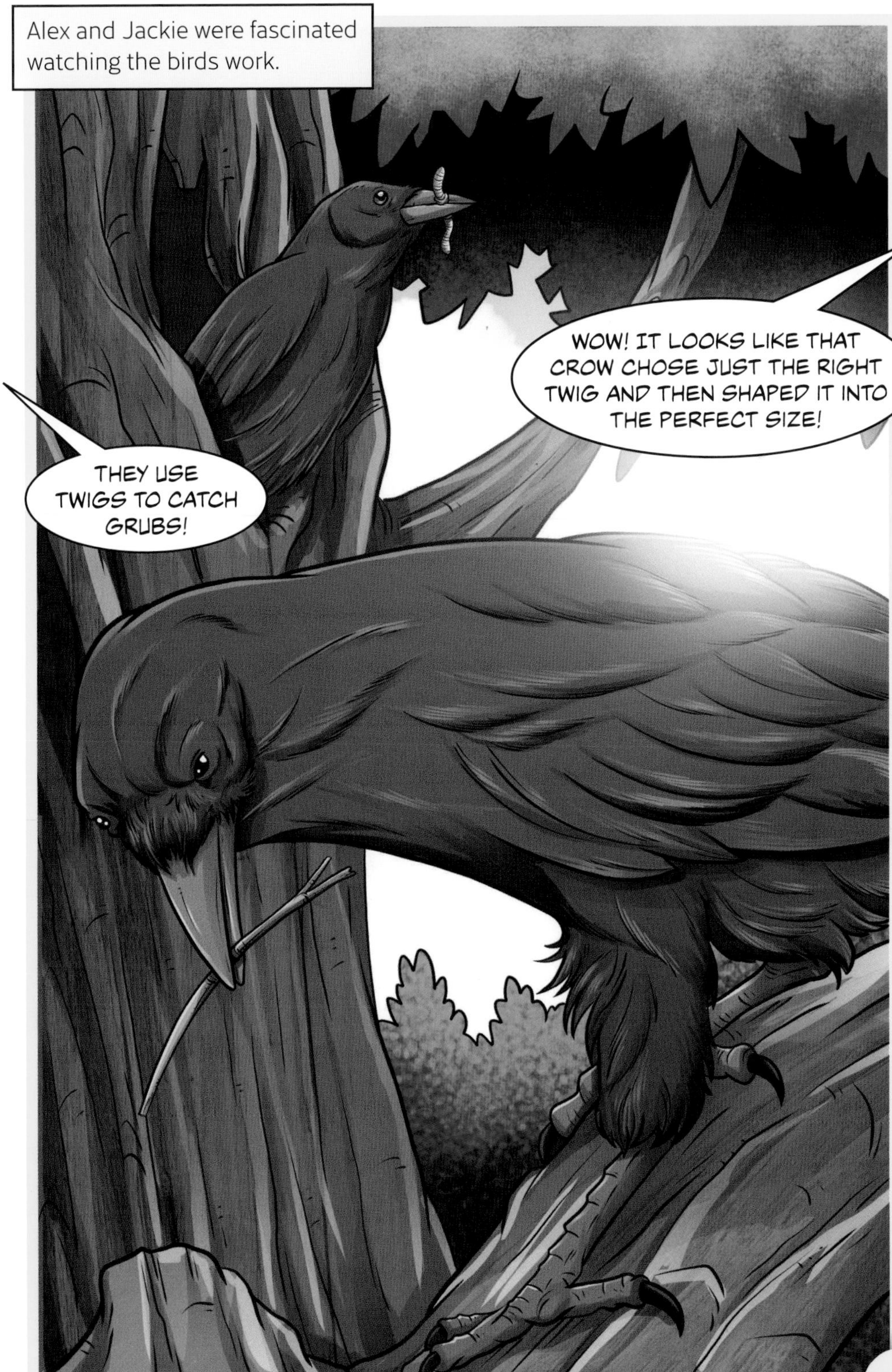
Alex and Jackie were fascinated watching the birds work.
THEY USE TWIGS TO CATCH GRUBS!
WOW! IT LOOKS LIKE THAT CROW CHOSE JUST THE RIGHT TWIG AND THEN SHAPED IT INTO THE PERFECT SIZE!

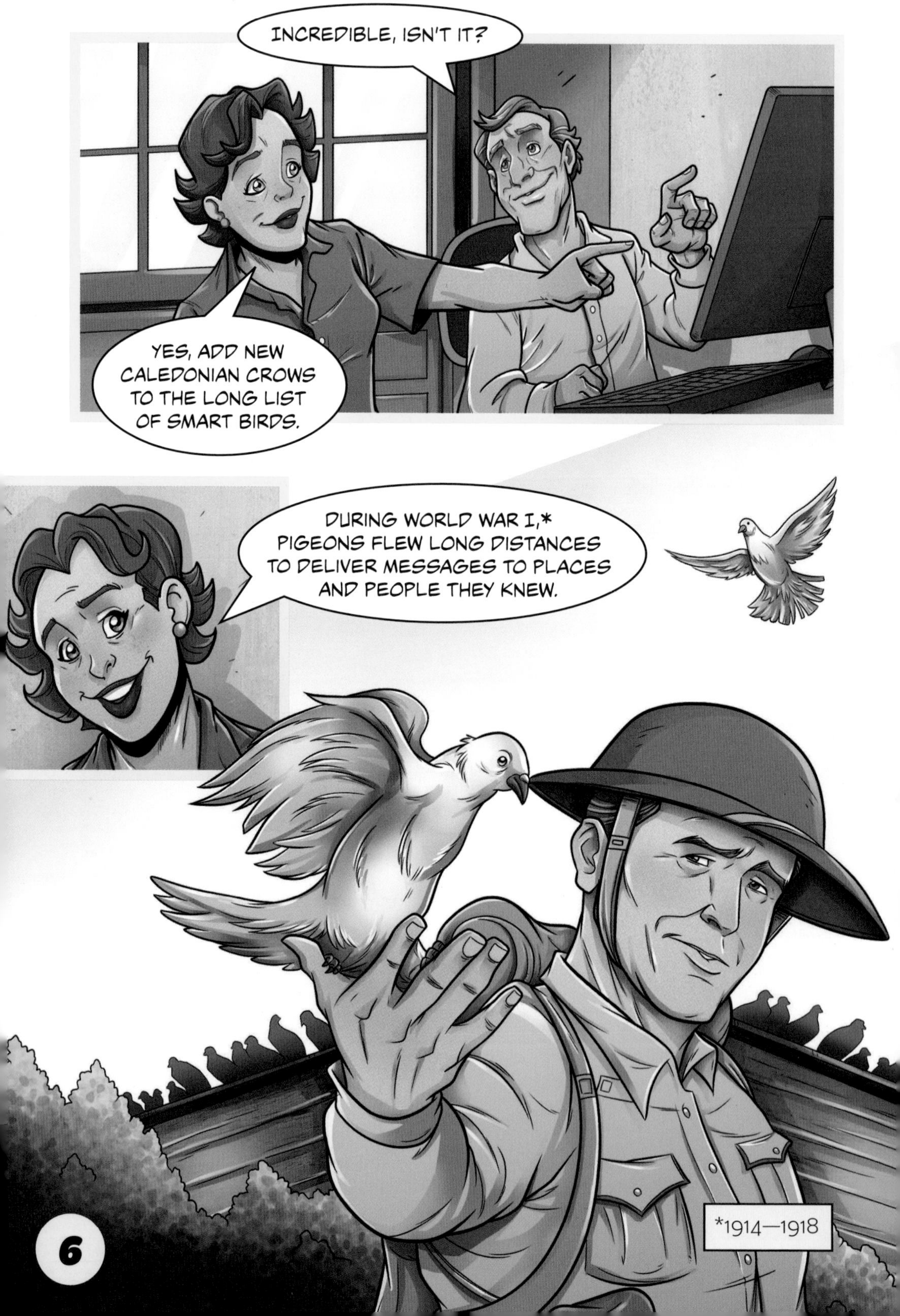
INCREDIBLE, ISN'T IT?
YES, ADD NEW CALEDONIAN CROWS TO THE LONG LIST OF SMART BIRDS.
DURING WORLD WAR I,* PIGEONS FLEW LONG DISTANCES TO DELIVER MESSAGES TO PLACES AND PEOPLE THEY KNEW.
*1914—1918

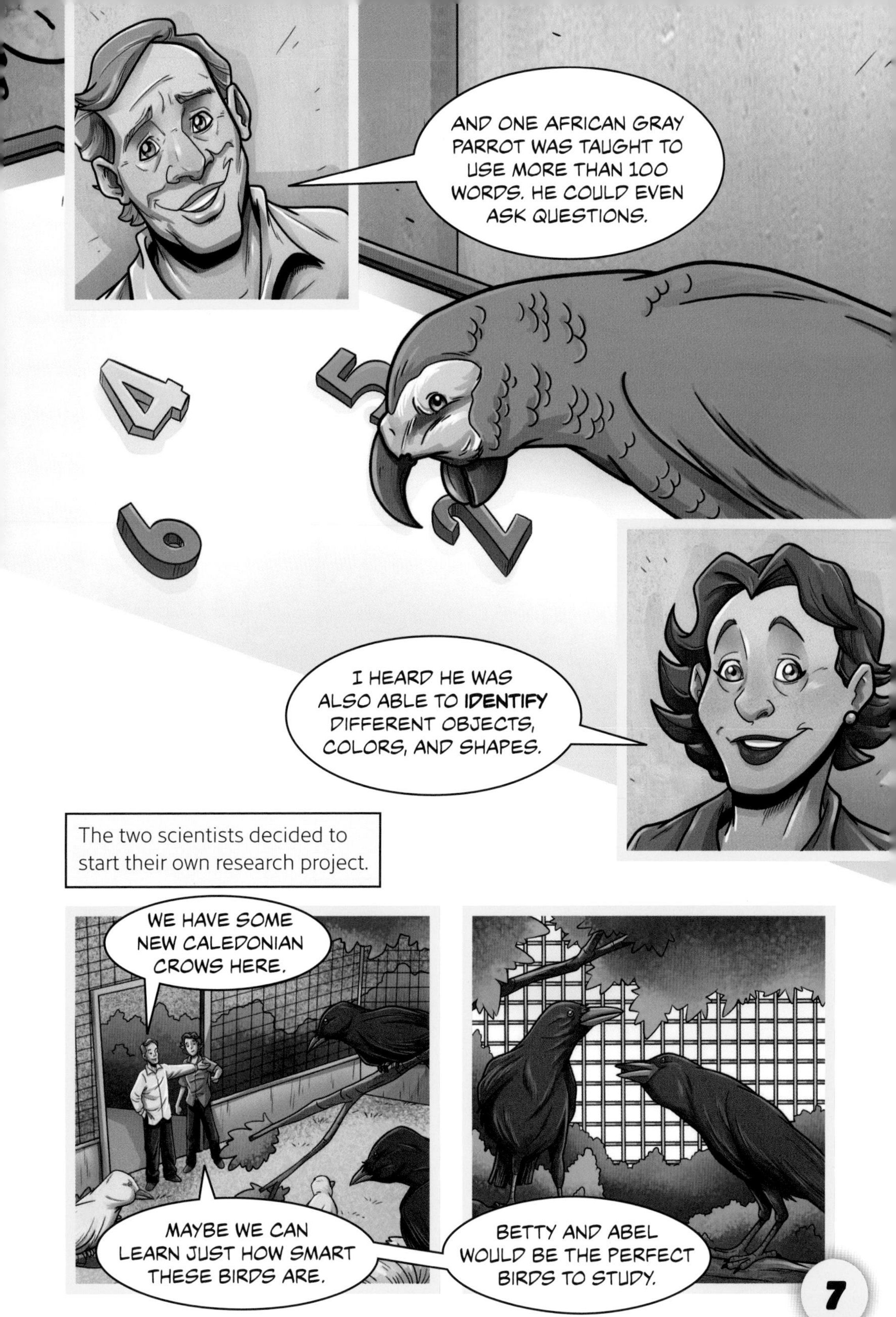
AND ONE AFRICAN GRAY PARROT WAS TAUGHT TO USE MORE THAN 100 WORDS. HE COULD EVEN ASK QUESTIONS.
I HEARD HE WAS ALSO ABLE TO **IDENTIFY** DIFFERENT OBJECTS, COLORS, AND SHAPES.
The two scientists decided to start their own research project.
WE HAVE SOME NEW CALEDONIAN CROWS HERE.
MAYBE WE CAN LEARN JUST HOW SMART THESE BIRDS ARE.
BETTY AND ABEL WOULD BE THE PERFECT BIRDS TO STUDY.

CHAPTER 2

Betty and Abel

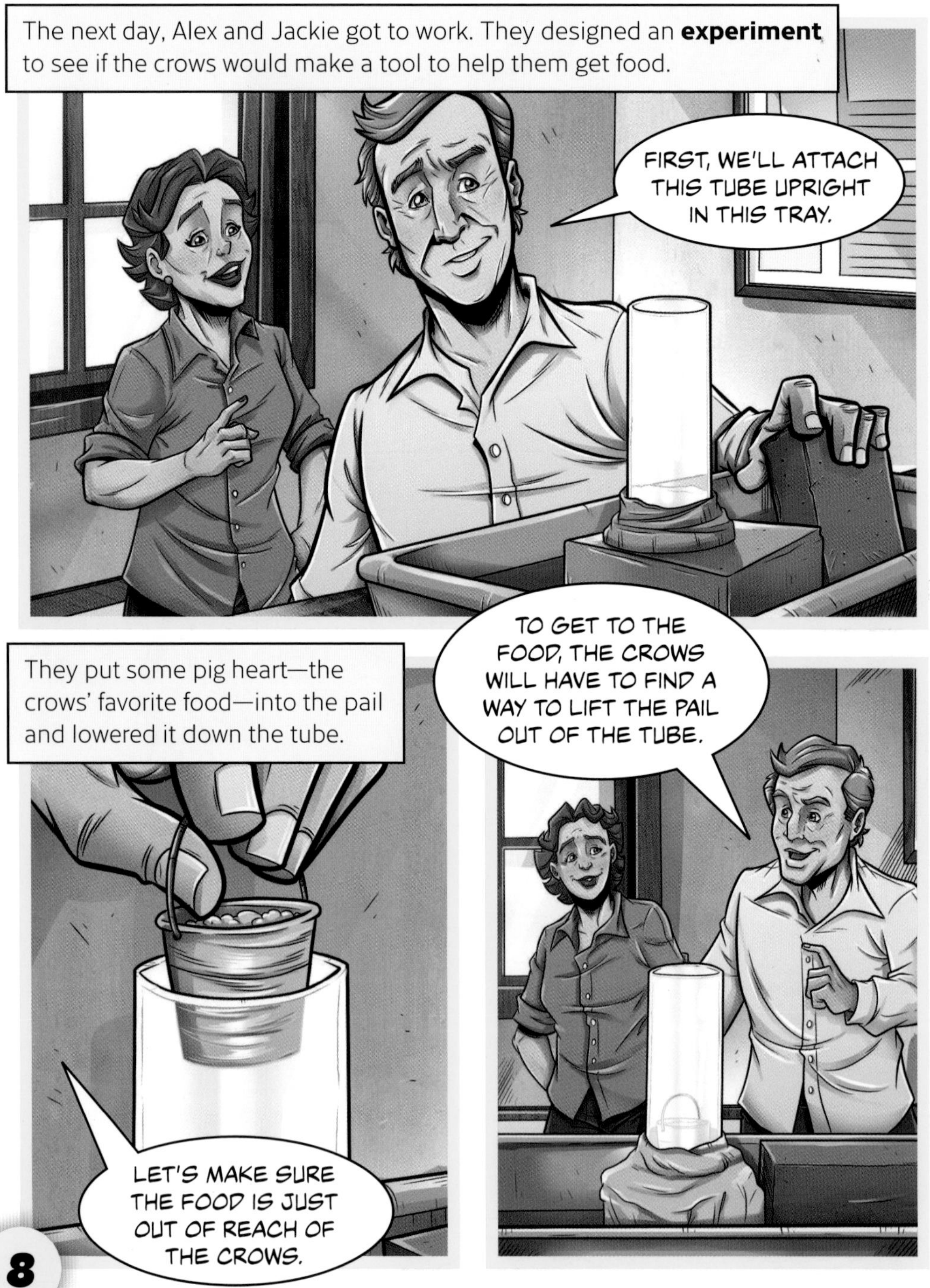
The next day, Alex and Jackie got to work. They designed an **experiment** to see if the crows would make a tool to help them get food.
FIRST, WE'LL ATTACH THIS TUBE UPRIGHT IN THIS TRAY.
They put some pig heart—the crows' favorite food—into the pail and lowered it down the tube.
LET'S MAKE SURE THE FOOD IS JUST OUT OF REACH OF THE CROWS.
TO GET TO THE FOOD, THE CROWS WILL HAVE TO FIND A WAY TO LIFT THE PAIL OUT OF THE TUBE.

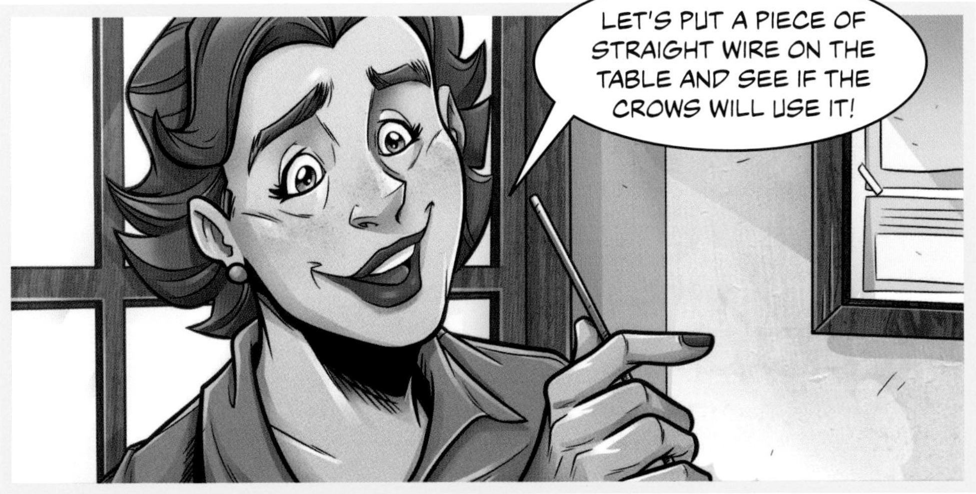
LET'S PUT A PIECE OF STRAIGHT WIRE ON THE TABLE AND SEE IF THE CROWS WILL USE IT!

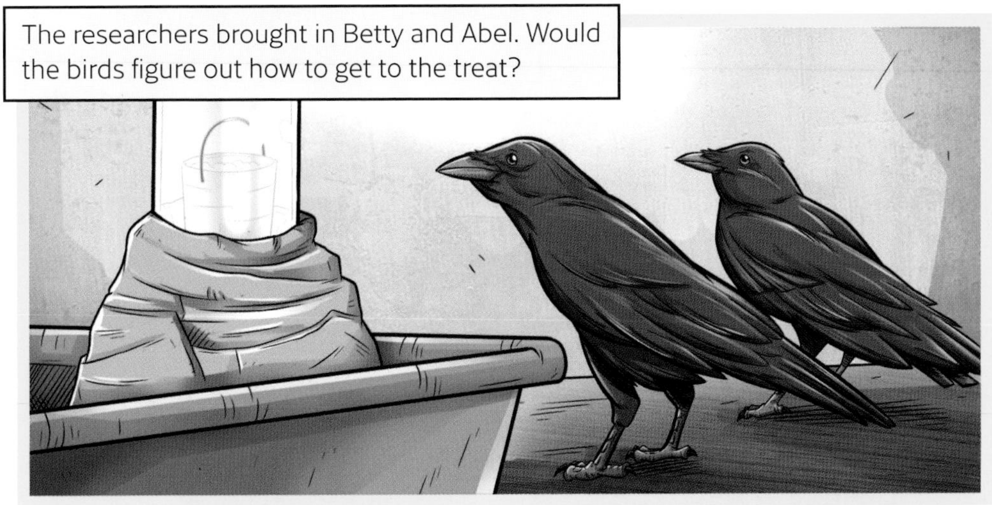
The researchers brought in Betty and Abel. Would the birds figure out how to get to the treat?

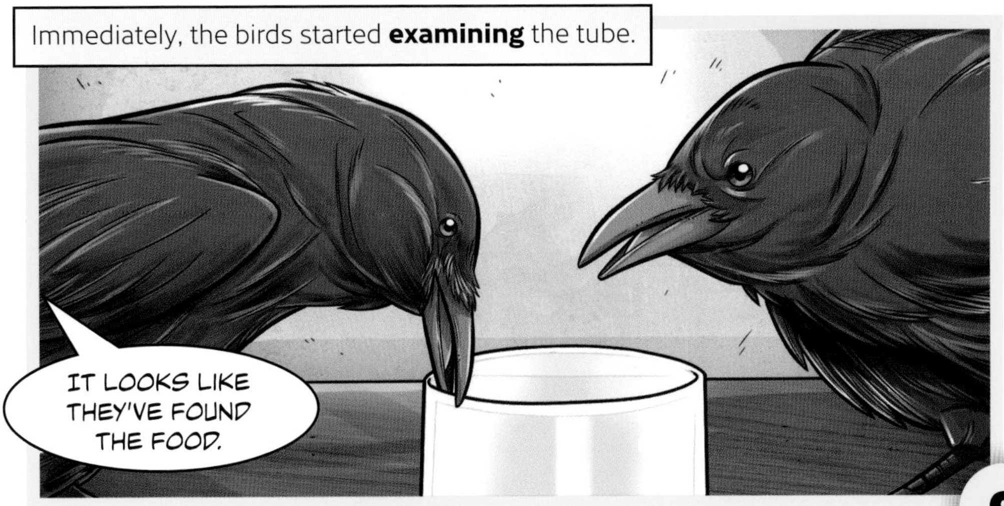
Immediately, the birds started **examining** the tube.
IT LOOKS LIKE THEY'VE FOUND THE FOOD.

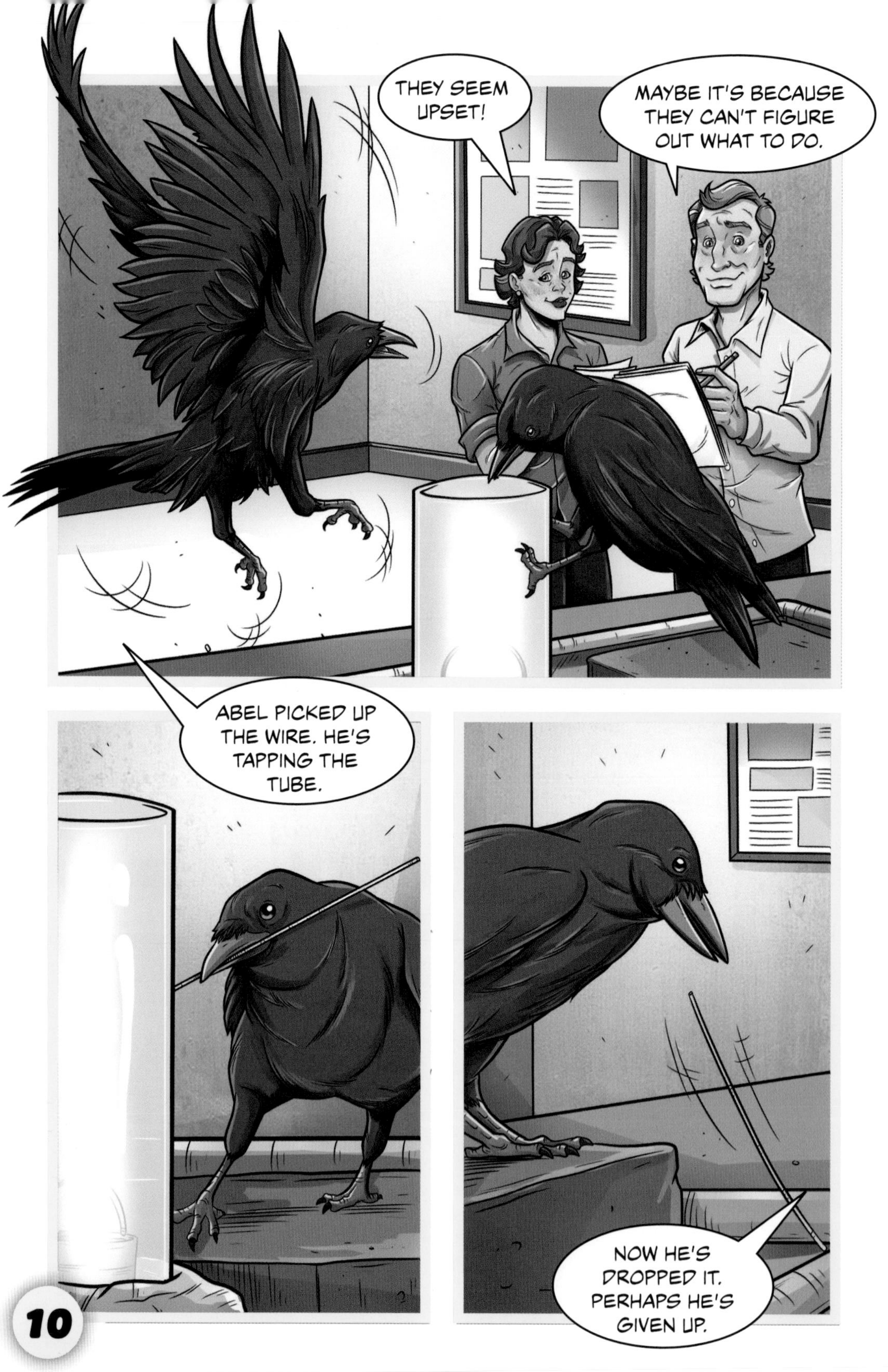
THEY SEEM UPSET!
MAYBE IT'S BECAUSE THEY CAN'T FIGURE OUT WHAT TO DO.
ABEL PICKED UP THE WIRE. HE'S TAPPING THE TUBE.
NOW HE'S DROPPED IT. PERHAPS HE'S GIVEN UP.

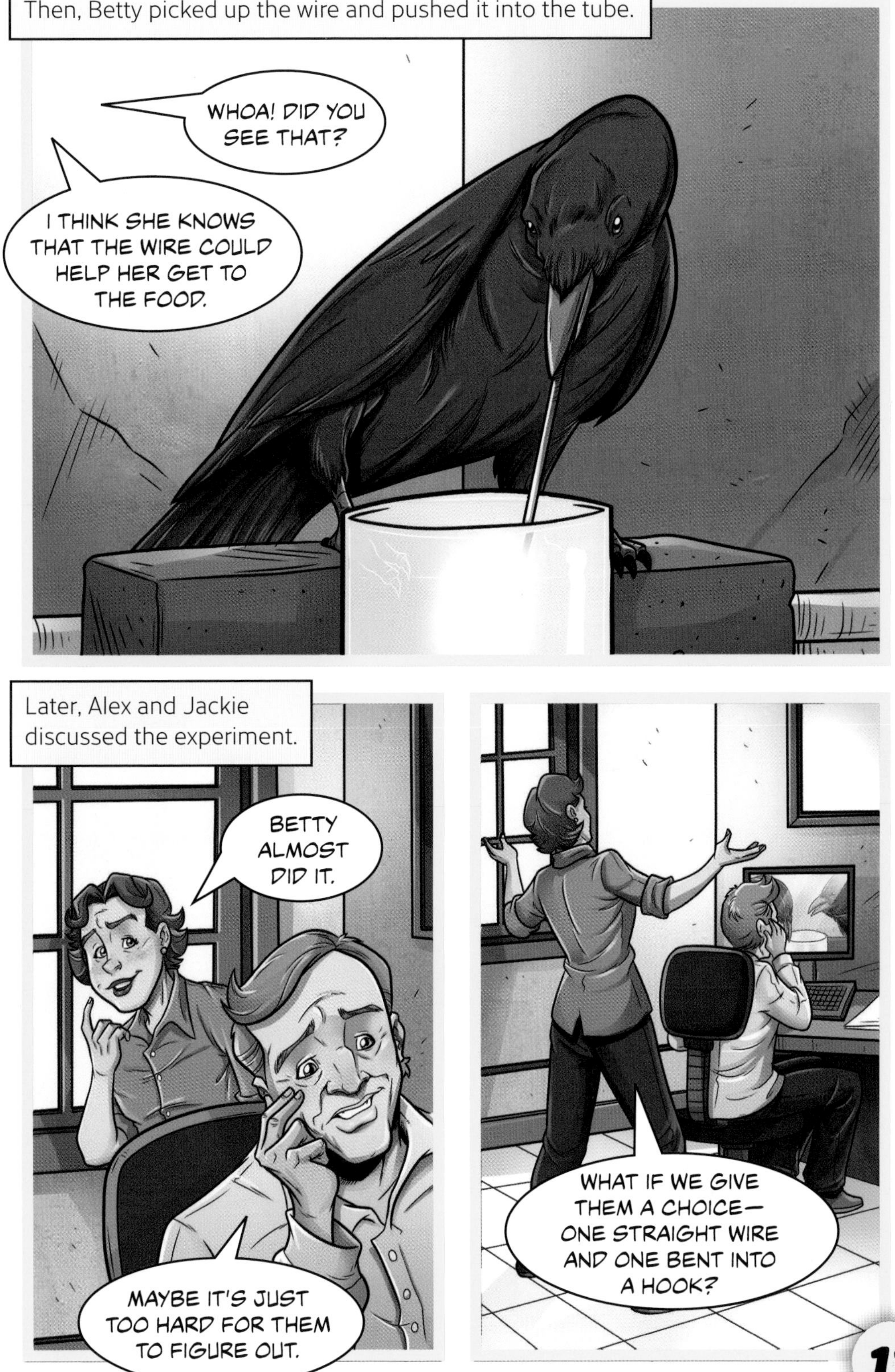
Then, Betty picked up the wire and pushed it into the tube.
WHOA! DID YOU SEE THAT?
I THINK SHE KNOWS THAT THE WIRE COULD HELP HER GET TO THE FOOD.
Later, Alex and Jackie discussed the experiment.
BETTY ALMOST DID IT.
MAYBE IT'S JUST TOO HARD FOR THEM TO FIGURE OUT.
WHAT IF WE GIVE THEM A CHOICE— ONE STRAIGHT WIRE AND ONE BENT INTO A HOOK?

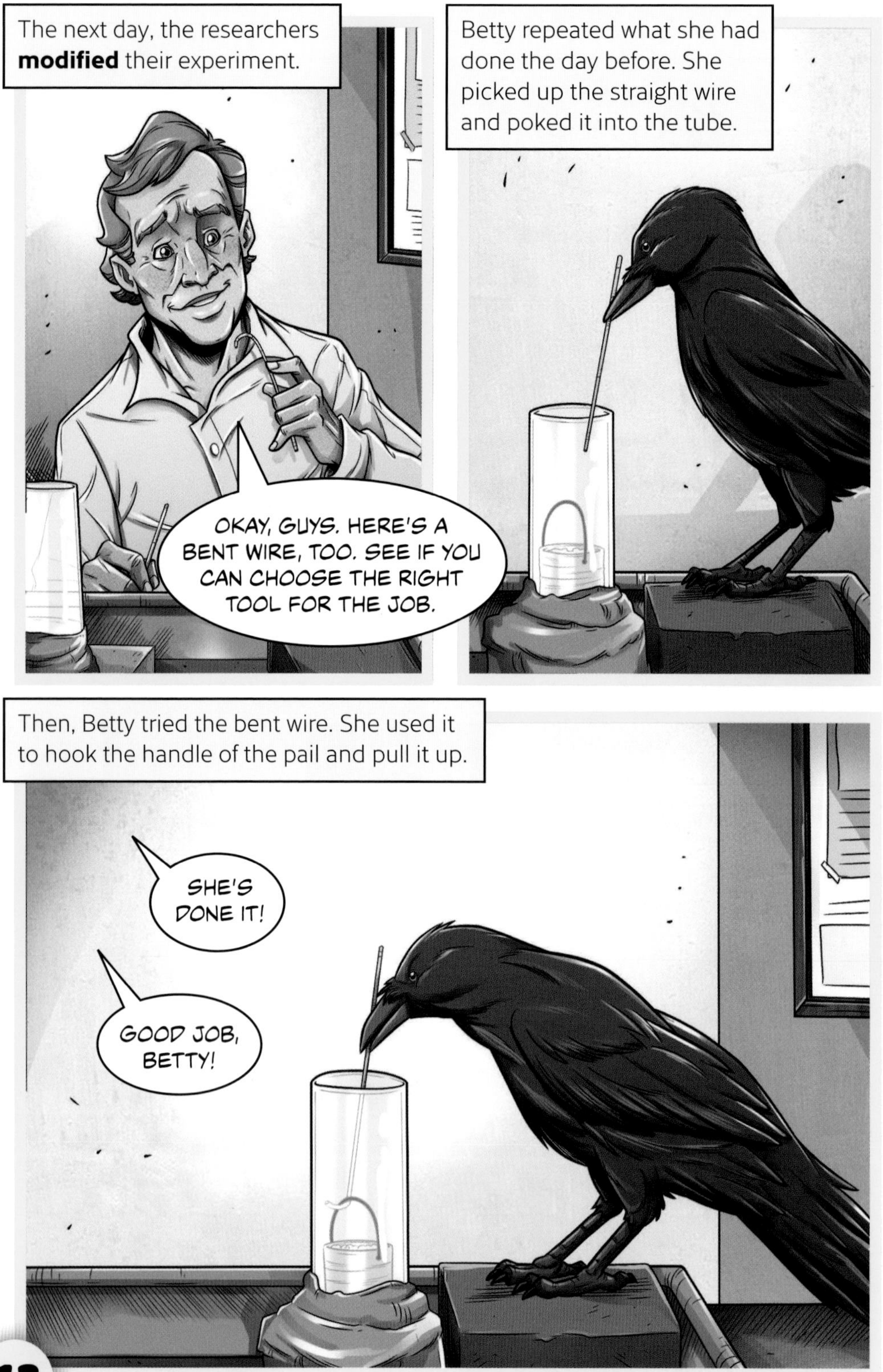
The next day, the researchers **modified** their experiment.
OKAY, GUYS. HERE'S A BENT WIRE, TOO. SEE IF YOU CAN CHOOSE THE RIGHT TOOL FOR THE JOB.
Betty repeated what she had done the day before. She picked up the straight wire and poked it into the tube.
Then, Betty tried the bent wire. She used it to hook the handle of the pail and pull it up.
SHE'S DONE IT!
GOOD JOB, BETTY!

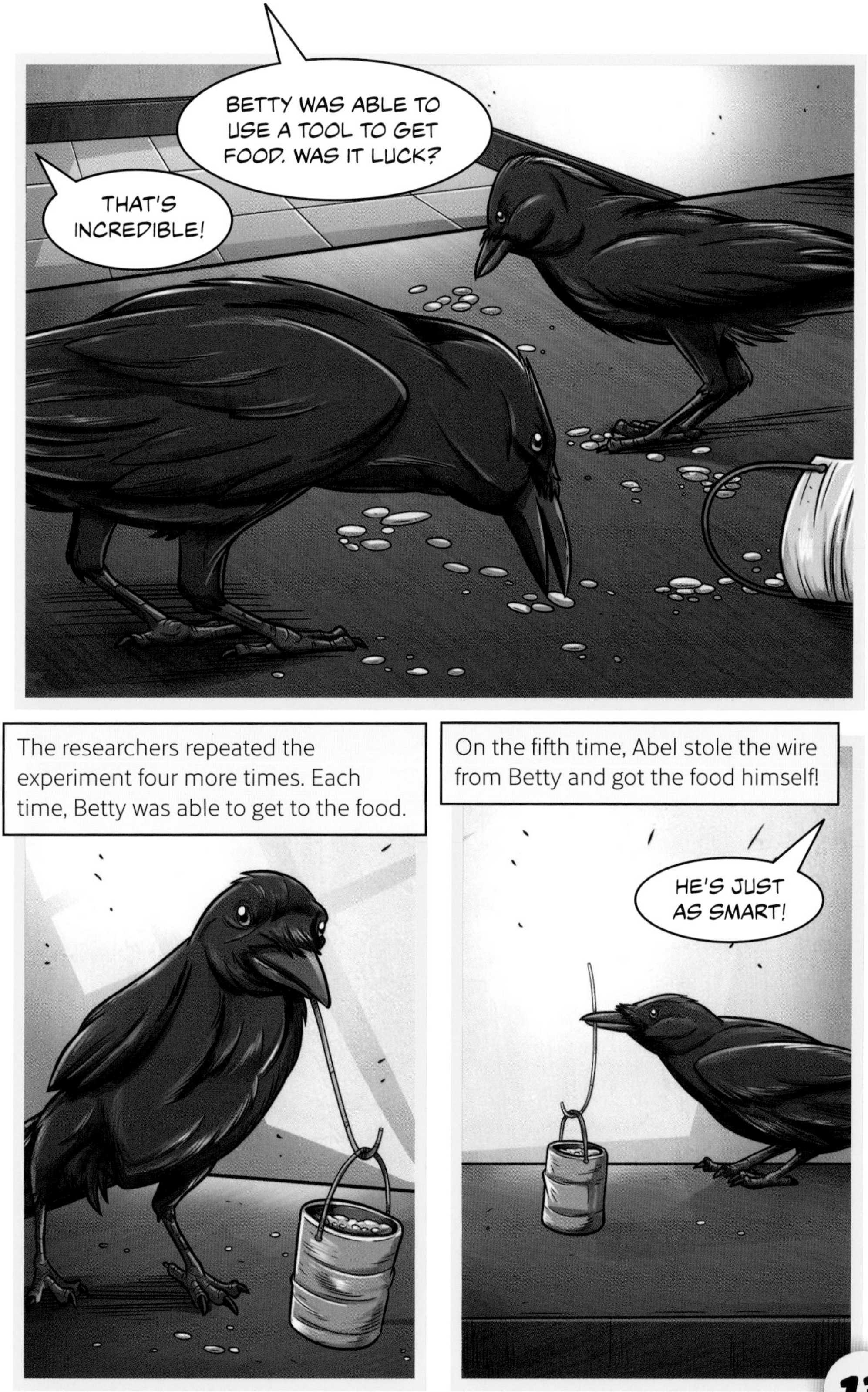
BETTY WAS ABLE TO USE A TOOL TO GET FOOD. WAS IT LUCK?
THAT'S INCREDIBLE!
The researchers repeated the experiment four more times. Each time, Betty was able to get to the food.
On the fifth time, Abel stole the wire from Betty and got the food himself!
HE'S JUST AS SMART!

CHAPTER 3

Smart Crows

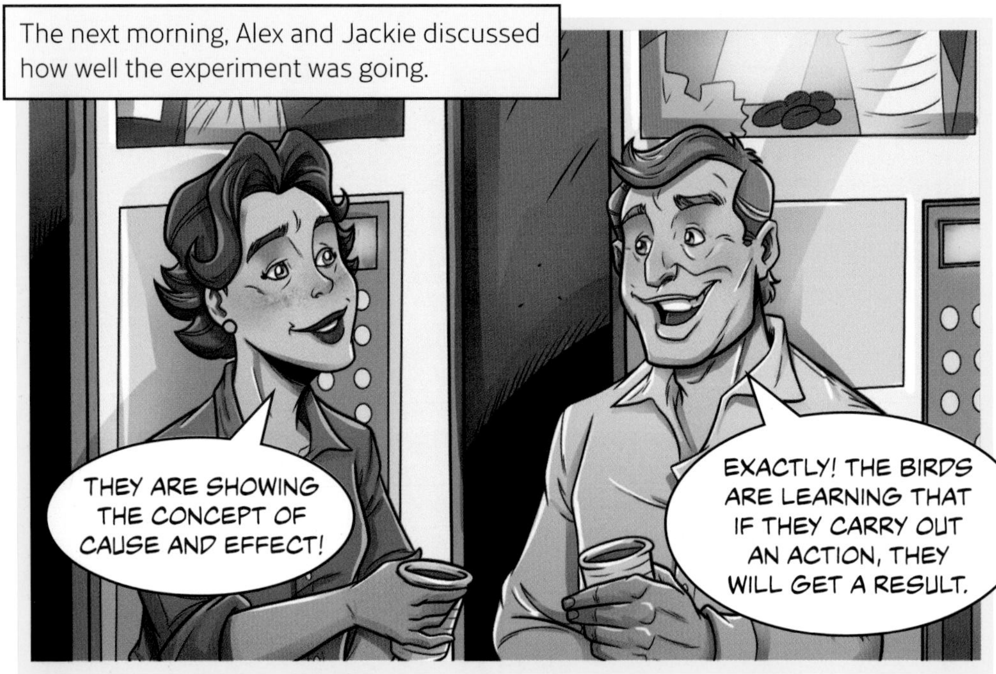
The next morning, Alex and Jackie discussed how well the experiment was going.
THEY ARE SHOWING THE CONCEPT OF CAUSE AND EFFECT!
EXACTLY! THE BIRDS ARE LEARNING THAT IF THEY CARRY OUT AN ACTION, THEY WILL GET A RESULT.

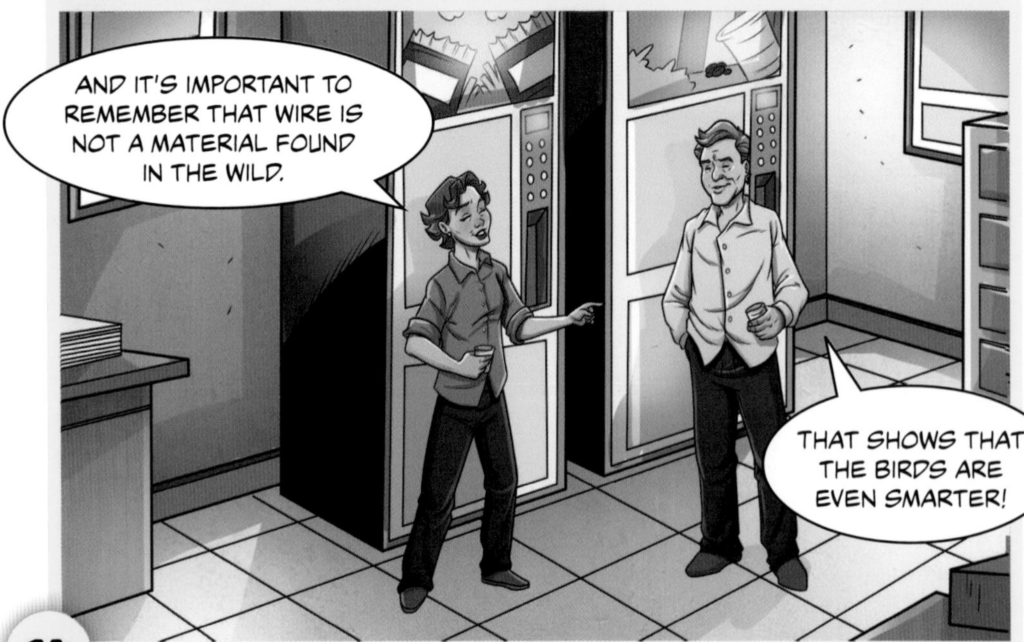
AND IT'S IMPORTANT TO REMEMBER THAT WIRE IS NOT A MATERIAL FOUND IN THE WILD.
THAT SHOWS THAT THE BIRDS ARE EVEN SMARTER!

The scientists continued their experiments to collect more **data**.

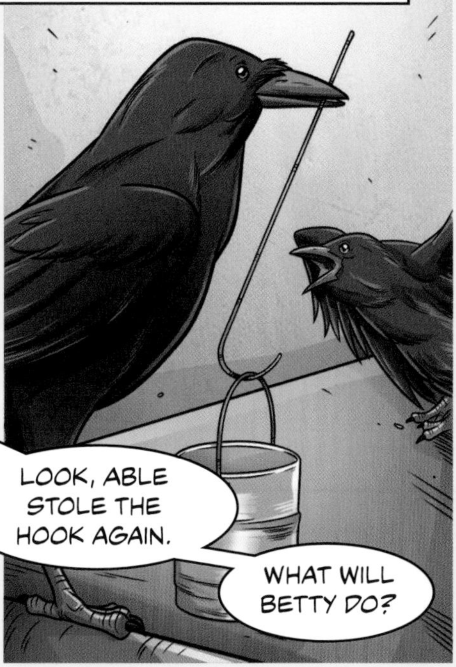
LOOK, ABLE STOLE THE HOOK AGAIN.
WHAT WILL BETTY DO?

Betty then picked up the straight wire and tried to use it to get the food.

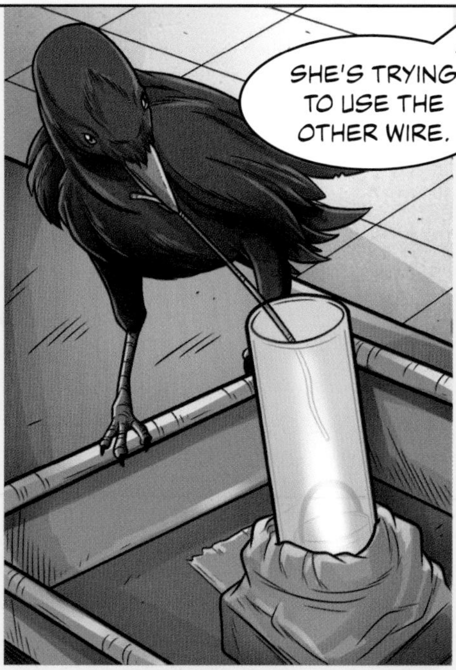
SHE'S TRYING TO USE THE OTHER WIRE.

The scientists were amazed by what happened next.

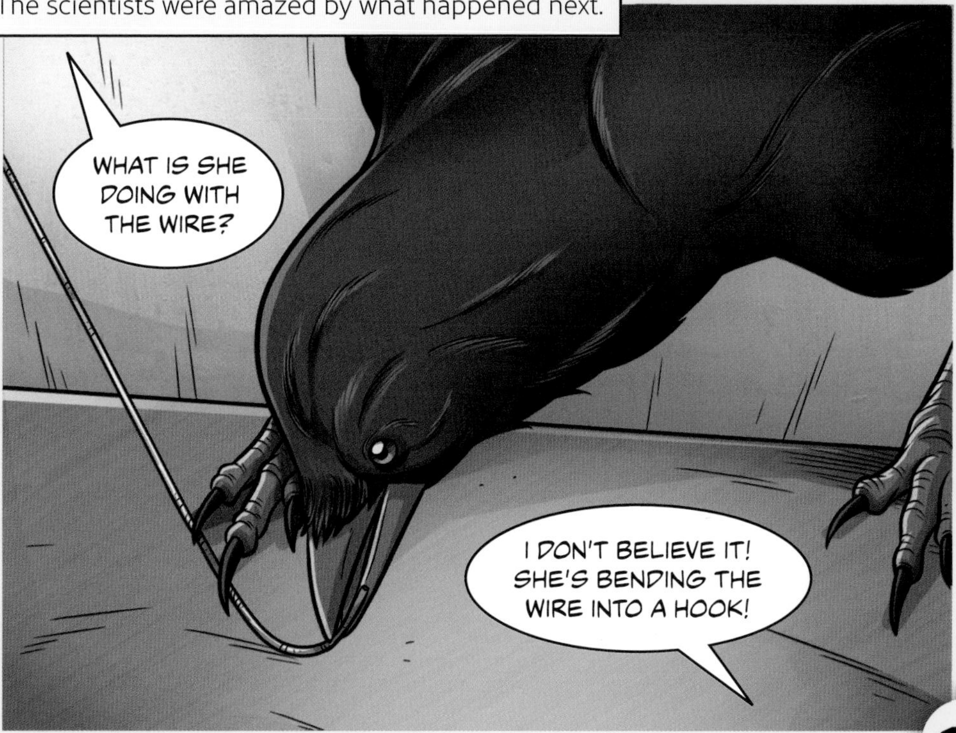
WHAT IS SHE DOING WITH THE WIRE?
I DON'T BELIEVE IT! SHE'S BENDING THE WIRE INTO A HOOK!

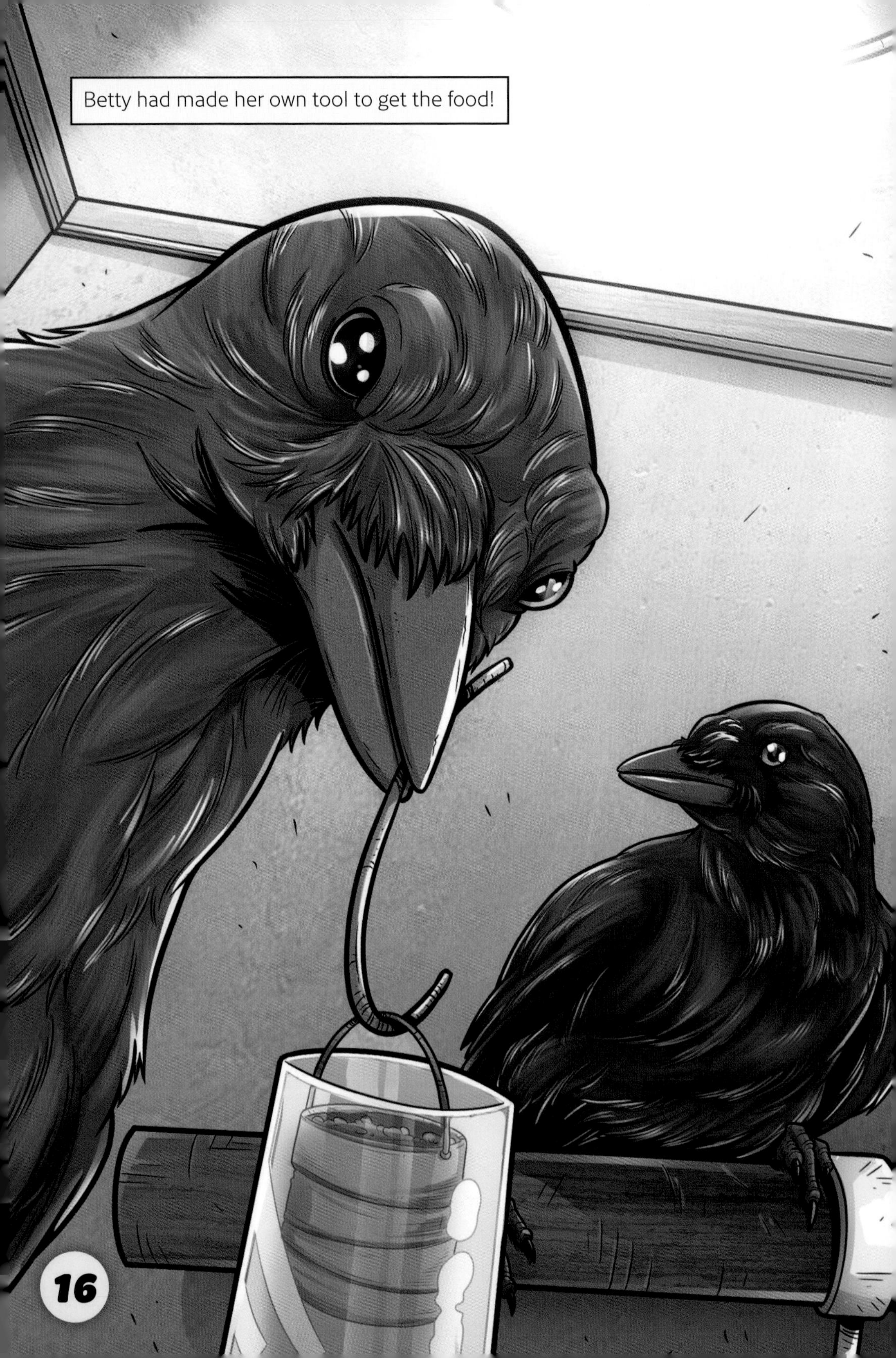
Betty had made her own tool to get the food!

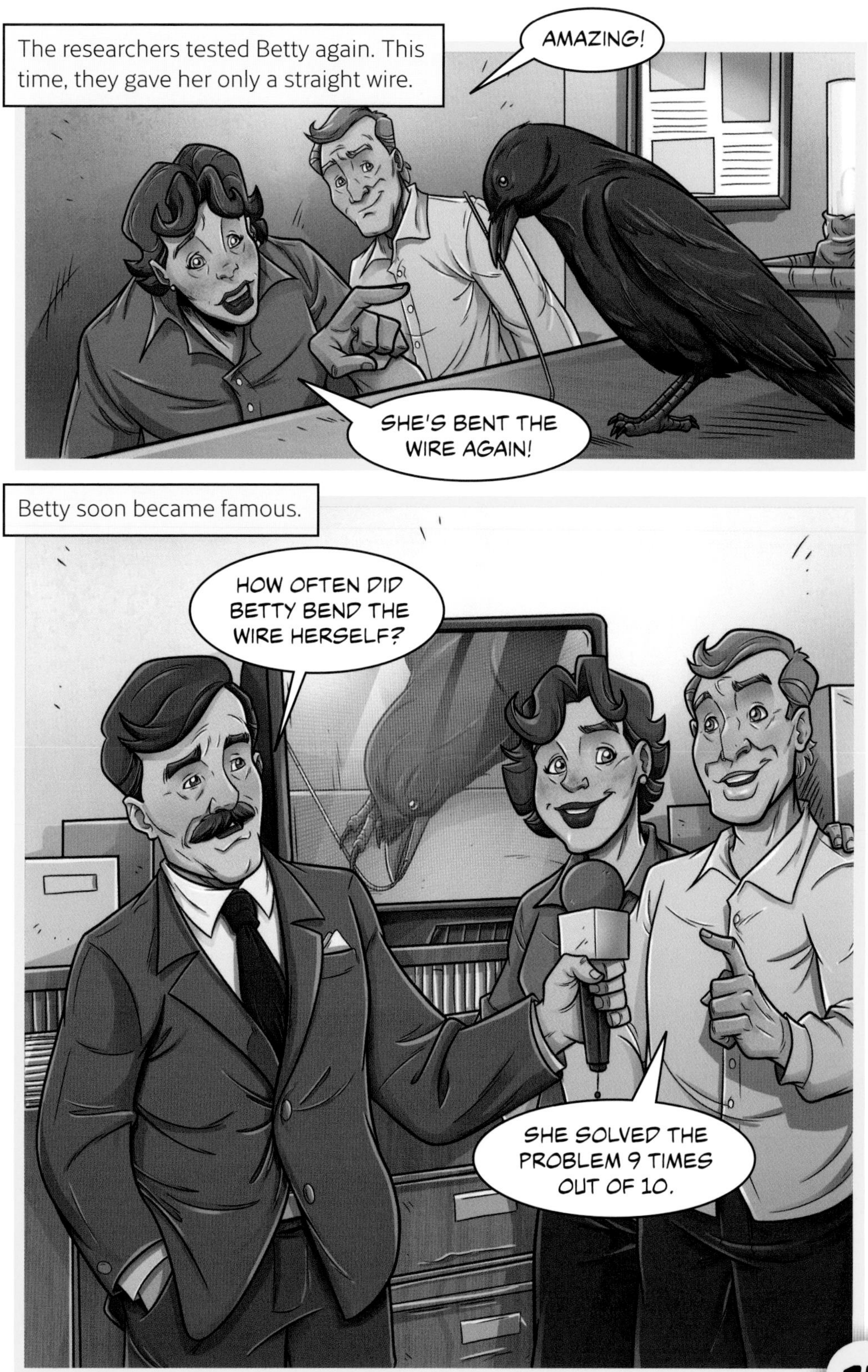
The researchers tested Betty again. This time, they gave her only a straight wire.
AMAZING!
SHE'S BENT THE WIRE AGAIN!
Betty soon became famous.
HOW OFTEN DID BETTY BEND THE WIRE HERSELF?
SHE SOLVED THE PROBLEM 9 TIMES OUT OF 10.

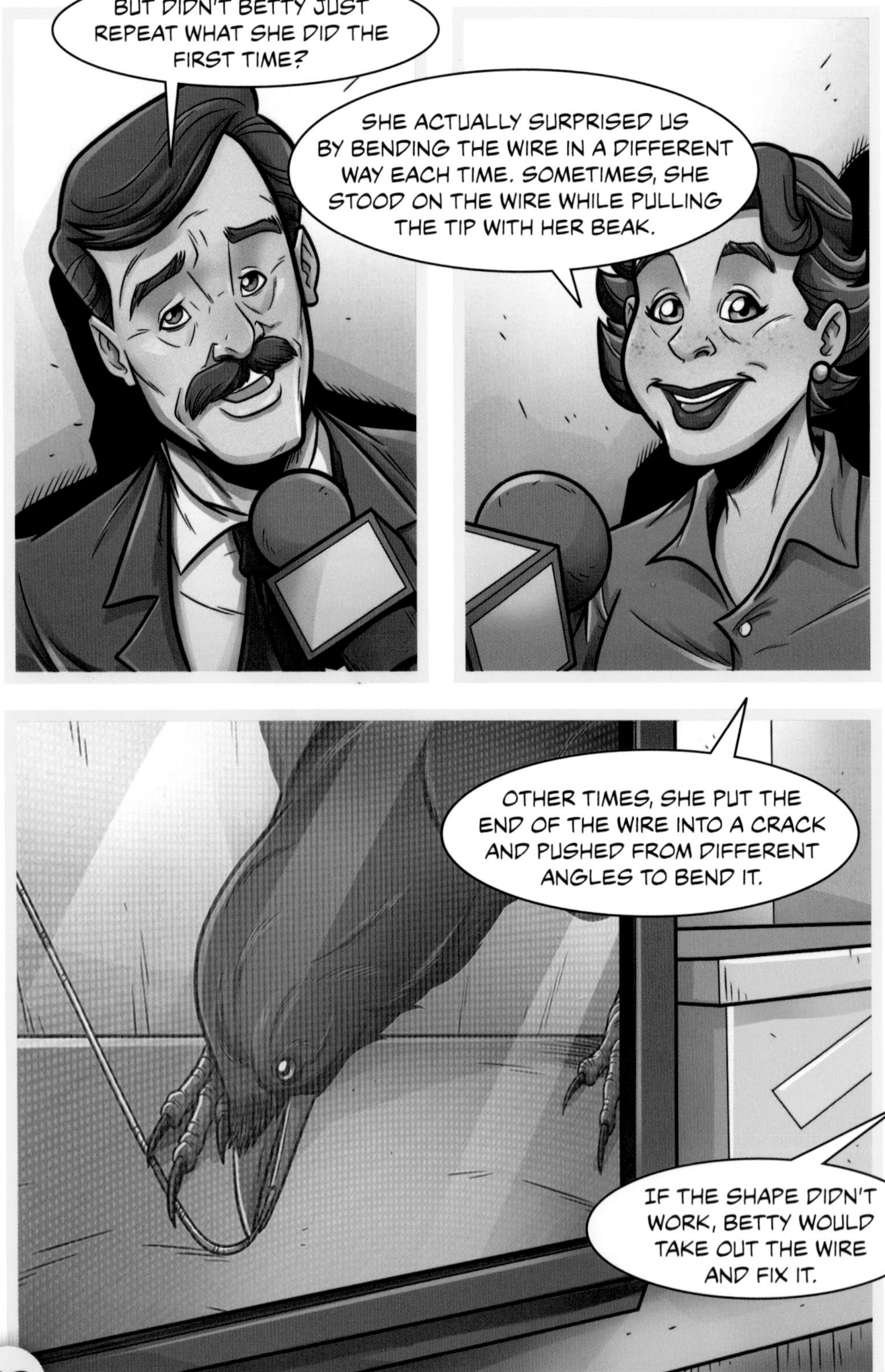
BUT DIDN'T BETTY JUST REPEAT WHAT SHE DID THE FIRST TIME?
SHE ACTUALLY SURPRISED US BY BENDING THE WIRE IN A DIFFERENT WAY EACH TIME. SOMETIMES, SHE STOOD ON THE WIRE WHILE PULLING THE TIP WITH HER BEAK.
OTHER TIMES, SHE PUT THE END OF THE WIRE INTO A CRACK AND PUSHED FROM DIFFERENT ANGLES TO BEND IT.
IF THE SHAPE DIDN'T WORK, BETTY WOULD TAKE OUT THE WIRE AND FIX IT.

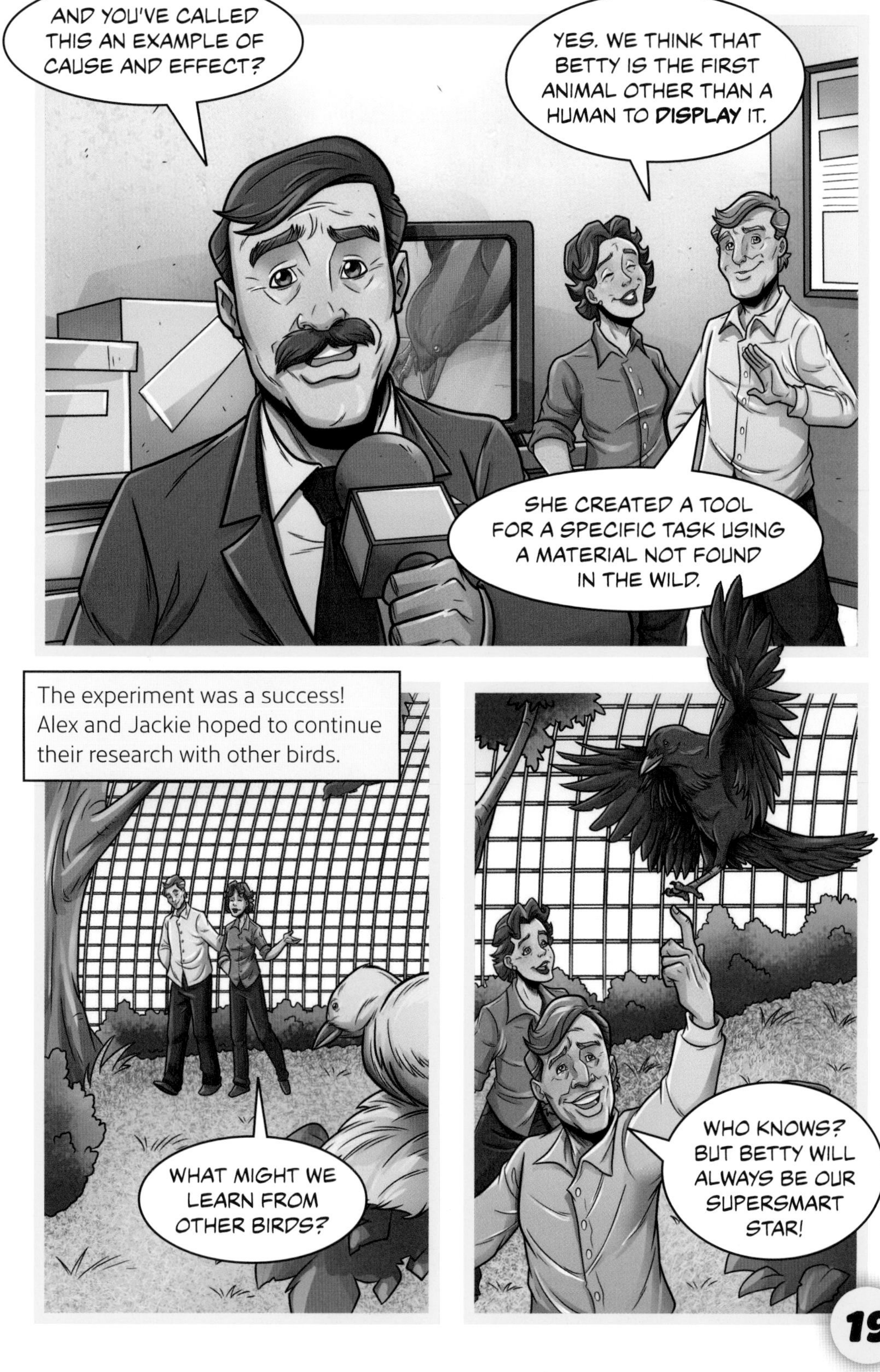
AND YOU'VE CALLED THIS AN EXAMPLE OF CAUSE AND EFFECT?
YES. WE THINK THAT BETTY IS THE FIRST ANIMAL OTHER THAN A HUMAN TO **DISPLAY** IT.
SHE CREATED A TOOL FOR A SPECIFIC TASK USING A MATERIAL NOT FOUND IN THE WILD.
The experiment was a success! Alex and Jackie hoped to continue their research with other birds.
WHAT MIGHT WE LEARN FROM OTHER BIRDS?
WHO KNOWS? BUT BETTY WILL ALWAYS BE OUR SUPERSMART STAR!

All about Crows

Crows are amazing birds that are known for their **intelligence**. These supersmart animals carefully watch everything that is going on around them. Some people have even taught crows to **mimic** speech.

- Crows eat many types of food. Their diet includes nuts, snails, eggs, lizards, insects, worms, and more.

CROWS LIVE IN FAMILY GROUPS WITH BABIES, OLDER **SIBLINGS**, AND THE PARENT BIRDS.

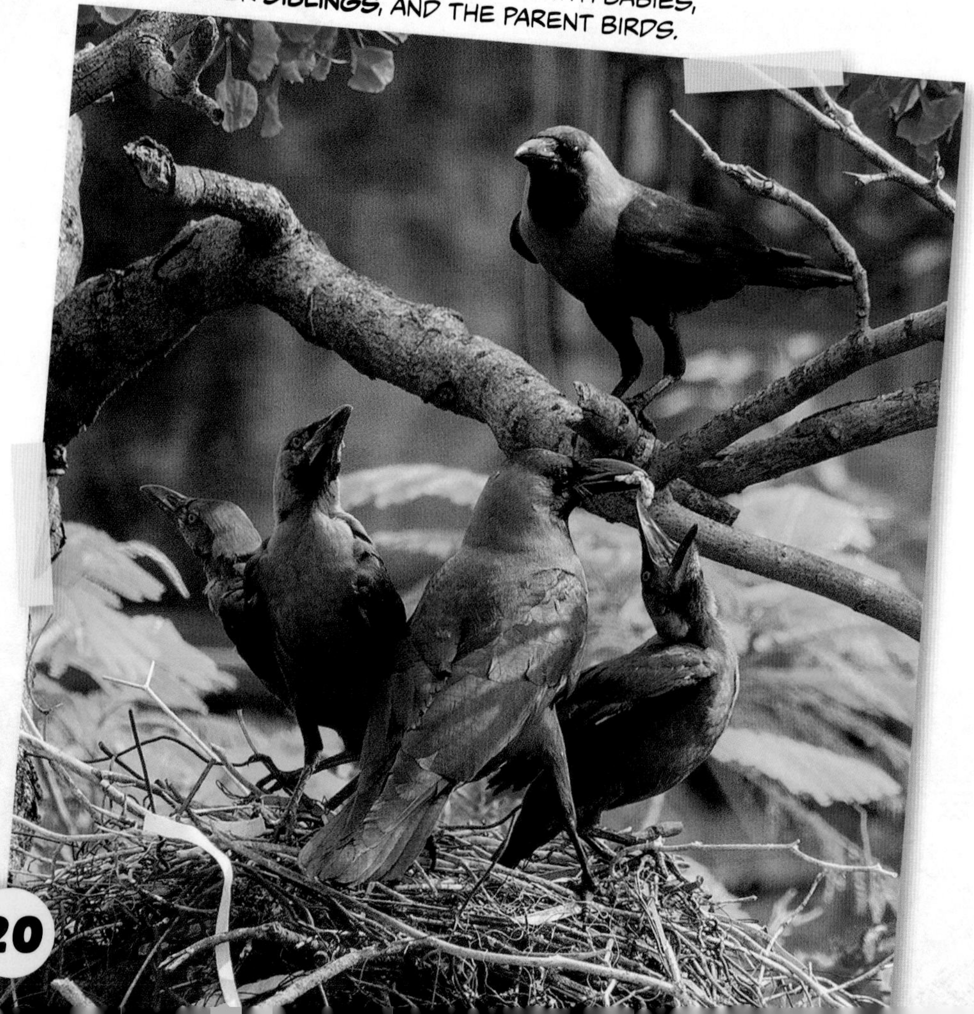

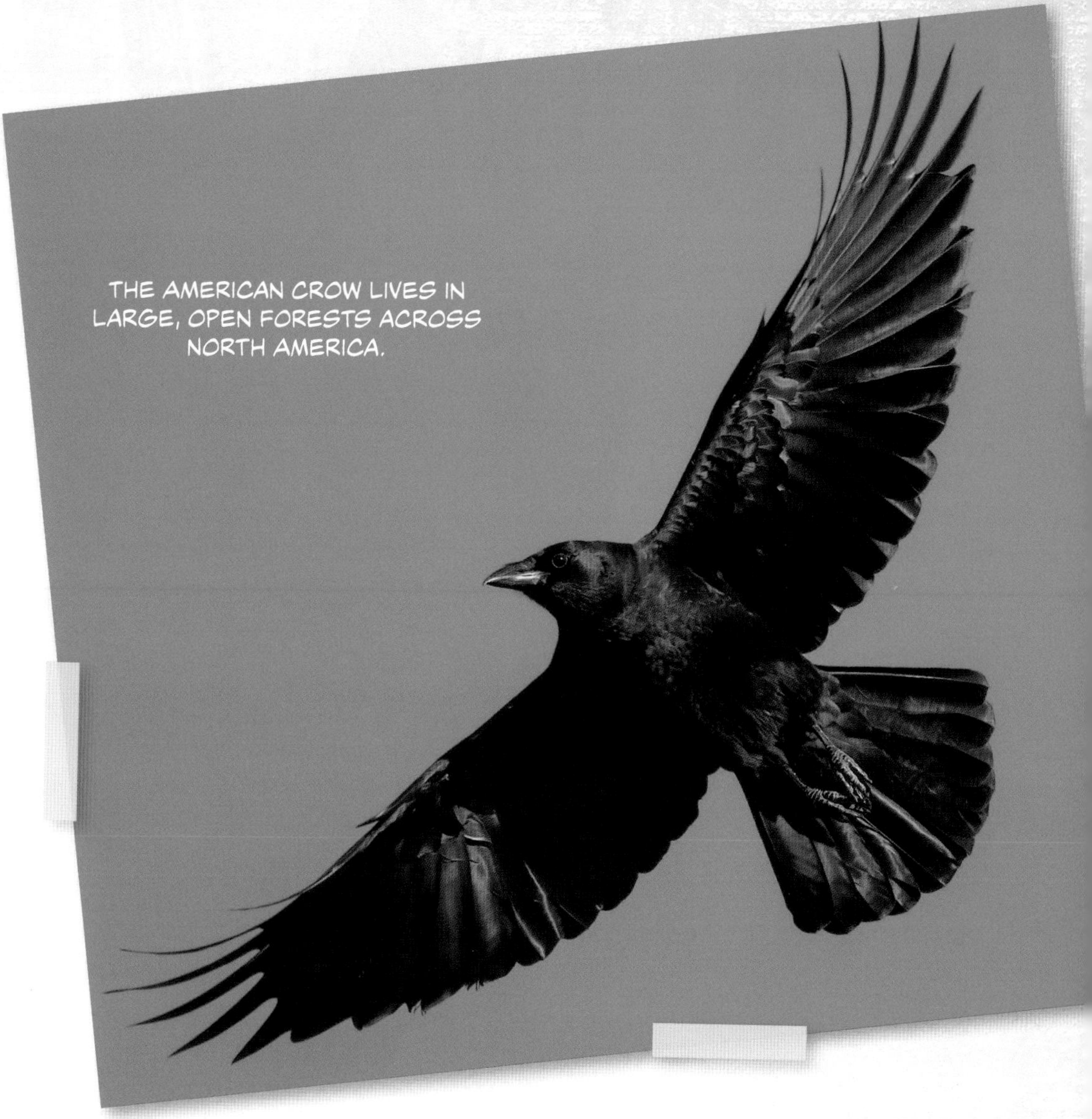

THE AMERICAN CROW LIVES IN LARGE, OPEN FORESTS ACROSS NORTH AMERICA.

- Crows use their strong beaks to catch small animals and insects. They can also use their beaks to break open shells.
- Crows live all over the world. They are found in North and Central America, northern Europe, and Asia. The birds typically live in wide-open places.
- Most crows in the wild can live for 15 to 20 years.

More Smart Crows

Much like the New Caledonian crows, Hawaiian ʻalalā crows have shown problem-solving smarts to get food. Researchers tested the crows' intelligence by drilling holes in a log. Scientists filled the holes with food and put sticks of different lengths nearby. Then, they stood back and watched what happened. Amazingly, the crows chose sticks exactly the right size to reach the food inside the log!

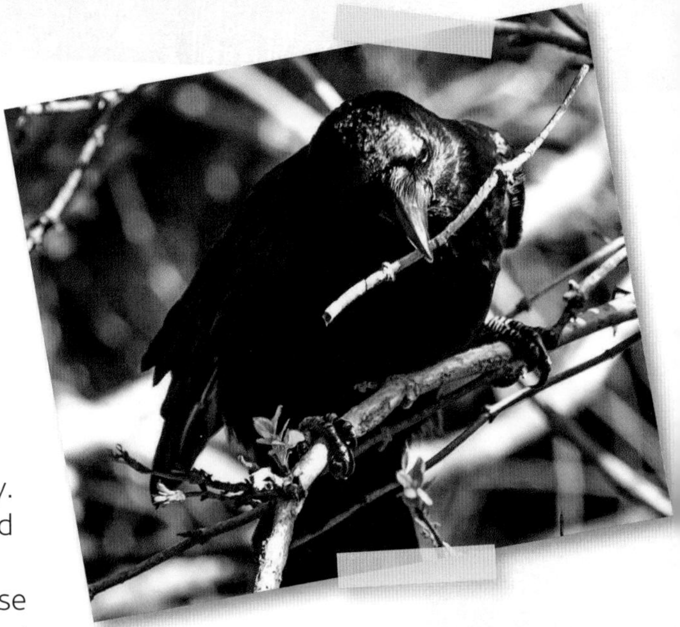

CROWS ARE ALSO SMART BUILDERS. THEY CHOOSE TWIGS THAT ARE THE RIGHT SIZE AND SHAPE FOR BUILDING A NEST.

Rook crows have also had their intelligence put to the test. Researchers challenged these crows to get a reward by raising the water in a container to bring food closer for the birds to access. One by one, the crows picked up stones the scientists had left around the container and placed them in the water. That made the water and the food rise. When it was within reach of the crows, the birds gobbled up the food and drank the water!

Glossary

data information

display to show

examining carefully looking at something

experiment a scientific procedure carried out to find out more about something

identify to correctly tell what something is

intelligence the ability to learn

mimic to copy something, such as sounds

modified changed

researcher a person who tries to find out more about something

siblings brothers and sisters

LIKE ALL CROWS, ROOKS CAN DO A LOT WITH THEIR BEAKS!

Index

African gray parrots 7
beaks 18, 21, 23
experiments 8, 11–15
food 8–9, 11–13, 15–16, 20, 22
intelligence 20, 22
mimicry 20

nests 22
pigeons 6
tools 4, 8, 12–13, 16, 19
twigs 4–5, 22
wires 9–15, 17–18

Read More

Garstecki, Julia. *Go Birding! (Wild Outdoors)*. North Mankato, MN: Capstone Press, 2022.

Jaycox, Jaclyn. *Unusual Life Cycles of Birds (Unusual Life Cycles)*. North Mankato, MN: Capstone Press, 2021.

Mattern, Joanne. *Crows (The World's Smartest Animals)*. Minneapolis: Bellwether Media, 2021.

Learn More Online

1. Go to **www.factsurfer.com** or scan the QR code below.
2. Enter "**Betty the Toolmaker**" into the search box.
3. Click on the cover of this book to see a list of websites.